An Illustrated Timeline of **SPACE EXPLORATION**

by Patricia Wooster
illustrated by Eldon Doty

PICTURE WINDOW BOOKS
a capstone imprint

Special thanks to our adviser, Terry Flaherty, PhD, Professor of English,
Minnesota State University, Mankato, for his expertise.

Editor: Jill Kalz
Designer: Tracy Davies
Art Director: Nathan Gassman
Production Specialist: Sarah Bennett
The illustrations in this book were created with ink and color wash.

Photo Credits: iStockphotos: parameter; Shutterstock: Markus Gann

Picture Window Books
151 Good Counsel Drive
P.O. Box 669
Mankato, MN 56002-0669
877-845-8392
www.capstonepub.com

All books published by Picture Window Books
are manufactured with paper containing at least
10 percent post-consumer waste.

Library of Congress Cataloging-in-Publication Data
Wooster, Patricia.
 An illustrated timeline of space exploration / by Patricia Wooster ;
illustrated by Eldon Doty.
      p. cm. — (Visual timelines in history)
 Includes index.
 ISBN 978-1-4048-6660-7 (library binding)
 ISBN 978-1-4048-7018-5 (paperback)
 1. Astronautics—History—Chronology—Juvenile literature. 2. Outer
space—Exploration—History—Chronology—Juvenile literature. I. Doty,
Eldon, ill. II. Title.
 TL793.W658 2012
 910.919'02—dc22
                        2011010466

Printed in the United States of America in North Mankato, Minnesota.
032011   006110CGF11

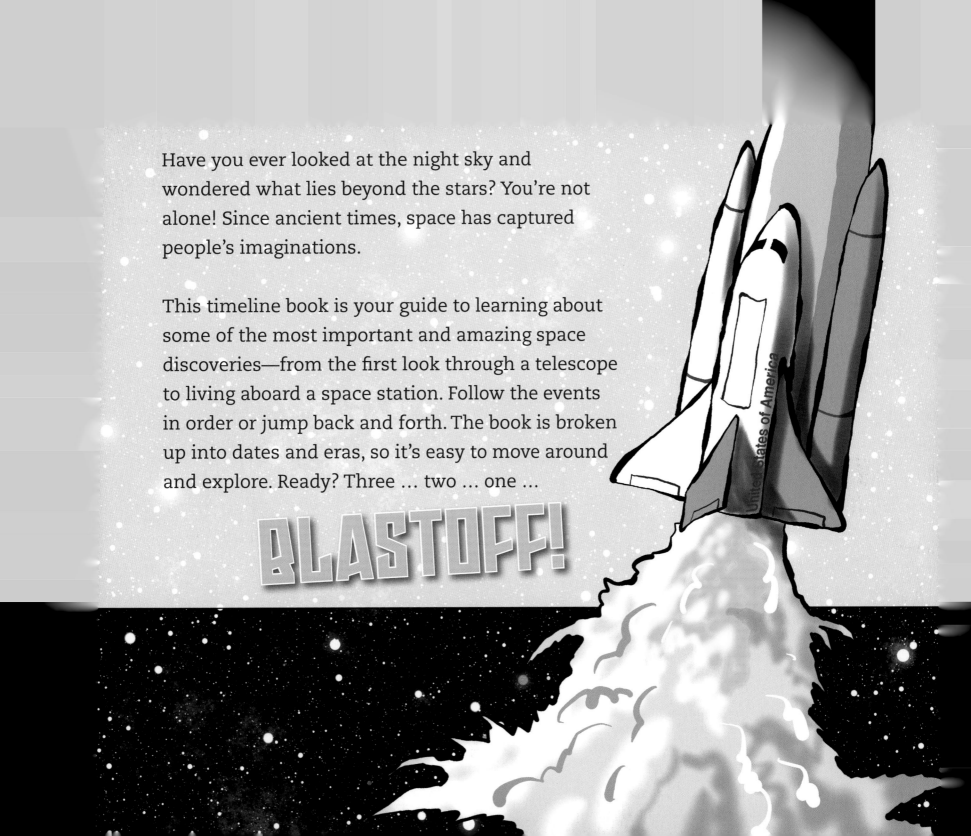

Have you ever looked at the night sky and wondered what lies beyond the stars? You're not alone! Since ancient times, space has captured people's imaginations.

This timeline book is your guide to learning about some of the most important and amazing space discoveries—from the first look through a telescope to living aboard a space station. Follow the events in order or jump back and forth. The book is broken up into dates and eras, so it's easy to move around and explore. Ready? Three ... two ... one ...

BLASTOFF!

EARLY DISCOVERIES

► 2773 BC

The Egyptians develop a 365-day calendar. It's based on the many stages, or phases, of the star Sirius.

1687

Sir Isaac Newton creates Newton's Laws. They are the three laws of motion for Earth, the other planets, and the moon.

AD 1543

Nicolaus Copernicus, an astronomer, says Earth is not the center of the universe. The sun is.

1609

Galileo Galilei creates his own telescope. He is able to look at the moon, discover four moons of Jupiter, and see a supernova.

1608

Hans Lippershey, a Dutch eyeglass maker, invents the first telescope. From now on, people can discover objects in the sky not seen with the naked eye.

1846

Johann Gottfried Galle, a German astronomer, discovers Neptune and its largest moon.

1847

William Herschel's son John, an astronomer, publishes a 164-page book about nebulas and stars.

1930

On February 18, Clyde Tombaugh, a farm boy from Kansas, discovers Pluto. Pluto is called a planet until 2006, when it's renamed a dwarf planet.

1781

Uranus is up here →

There's a bunch of stars down here →

a little star here →

William Herschel, an English astronomer, discovers Uranus and maps the stars.

1929

Edwin Powell Hubble creates Hubble's Law. This law gives proof of an expanding universe, meaning space is growing bigger every day.

THE SPACE AGE

October 4, 1957

The Soviet Union launches the world's first artificial satellite. Called *Sputnik 1*, it signals the start of the Space Age. *Sputnik 1* is the size of a beach ball.

January 31, 1958

The United States launches its first satellite, called *Explorer 1*.

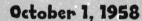

October 1, 1958

The National Aeronautics and Space Administration (NASA) is founded. Its mission is to lead the United States into space exploration.

November 3, 1957

A dog named Laika (later nicknamed "Muttnik") is the first living creature to be launched into space. It travels aboard the Soviet space satellite *Sputnik 2*.

September 12, 1959

The Soviet spacecraft *Luna* 2 crashes into the moon. It becomes the first craft to land on another object in space.

October 10, 1960

The Soviet Union tries to launch a probe to fly by Mars. The craft reaches just 75 miles (120 km) before falling back to Earth.

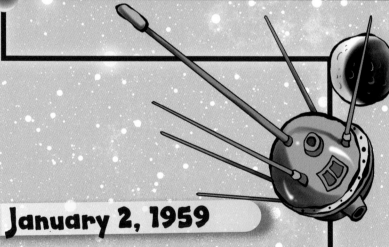

October 4, 1959

The Soviet *Luna* 3 becomes the third spacecraft launched to the moon. It does a flyby and is the first to send photos of the moon to Earth.

January 2, 1959

A Soviet spacecraft called *Luna* 1 is the first craft to fly by the moon. It discovers the moon has no magnetic field.

THE SPACE RACE

▶ January 31, 1961

A chimpanzee named Ham rides aboard a *Mercury* space capsule launched by the United States. The flight lasts 16.5 minutes.

May 25, 1961

U.S. President John F. Kennedy issues a nationwide challenge. He wants to land "a man on the moon and return him safely to Earth" before 1970.

April 12, 1961

Cosmonaut Yuri Gagarin becomes the first human in space and the first person to orbit Earth.

May 5, 1961

Alan Shepard becomes the first American in space. He completes a 15-minute flight aboard *Freedom 7*.

July 10, 1962

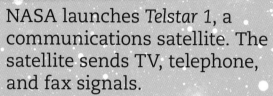

NASA launches *Telstar 1*, a communications satellite. The satellite sends TV, telephone, and fax signals.

October 12, 1964

The Soviet Union launches *Voskhod 1*. It's the first spacecraft to carry multiple crew members.

February 20, 1962

John Glenn becomes the first U.S. astronaut to orbit Earth.

June 16, 1963

Cosmonaut Valentina Tereshkova orbits Earth 48 times. She is the first woman to travel in space.

TESTING THE SKIES

March 18, 1965

Cosmonaut Alexei Leonov completes the first space walk. It lasts 12 minutes.

July 14, 1965

The U.S. probe *Mariner 4* takes the first photographs of Mars from space.

Mars: 21178

Mars: 2

June 3, 1965

Astronaut Edward White II becomes the first American to walk in space.

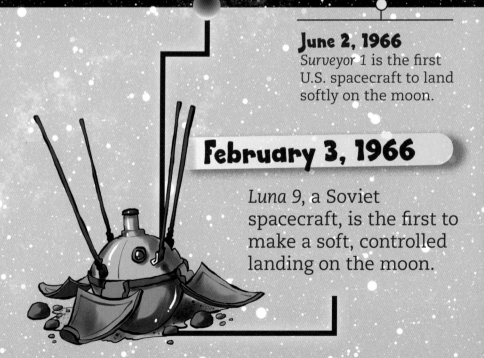

June 2, 1966
Surveyor 1 is the first U.S. spacecraft to land softly on the moon.

February 3, 1966

Luna 9, a Soviet spacecraft, is the first to make a soft, controlled landing on the moon.

October 18, 1967

The Soviet probe *Venera 4* is the first spacecraft to enter the atmosphere of Venus.

October 19, 1967

The U.S. probe *Mariner 5* reports a high amount of carbon dioxide and no magnetic field on Venus.

December 24, 1968

Launched by the United States, *Apollo 8* is the first manned spacecraft to orbit the moon. Over 66 hours, it travels 230,000 miles (370,149 km).

September 18, 1968

The Soviet probe *Zond 5* is the first spacecraft to orbit the moon. It carries a cargo of turtles, flies, and a mannequin.

WALKING ON THE MOON

▶ July 20, 1969

U.S. astronaut Neil Armstrong becomes the first person to walk on the moon, followed by crewmate Buzz Aldrin. Both are part of the *Apollo 11* mission.

OXYGEN TANK 2

KABOOM!

April 11, 1970

Apollo 13 is launched by the United States. Fifty-six hours later, an oxygen tank explodes, and the crew uses the lunar module to return to Earth.

September 20, 1970

The Soviet probe *Luna 16* collects a moon sample and returns it to Earth. It is the world's first fully robotic sample return.

CCCP

December 15, 1970

The Soviet probe *Venera 7* is the first probe to land on Venus.

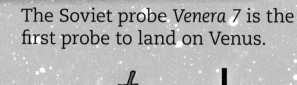

November 13, 1971

The U.S. probe *Mariner 9* becomes the first spacecraft to orbit Mars.

July 30, 1971

U.S. astronauts David Scott and James Irwin drive the first vehicle on the moon. They are members of the *Apollo* 15 mission.

April 19, 1971

The Soviet *Salyut 1* becomes the world's first space station. Its first crew members arrive June 7.

ANOTHER STATION IN SPACE

Cygnus X-1 is here, but you can't see it because it is a black hole.

1972

Cygnus X-1 is named the first black hole.

July 15, 1972

The U.S. spacecraft *Pioneer 10* becomes the first craft to fly through an asteroid belt. It was launched on March 2.

December 14, 1972

Apollo 17, launched by the United States, is the last manned mission to the moon.

LUNAR ROVING VEHICLE

May 14, 1973

The United States launches its first space station, *Skylab*. The first U.S. crew visits 11 days later.

October 22, 1975

The Soviet spacecraft *Venera* 9 lands on Venus and sends the first pictures from the planet's surface.

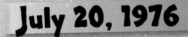

1975

The European Space Agency (ESA) is founded. Its mission is to lead countries within Europe into space research.

March 29, 1974

The U.S. probe *Mariner 10* is the first spacecraft to fly past Mercury.

July 20, 1976

The U.S. probe *Viking* 1 is the first spacecraft to land on Mars.

July 17, 1975

Apollo 18 astronauts and *Soyuz 19* cosmonauts dock their spacecraft together in space.

REACHING FARTHER INTO SPACE

JUPITER

SATURN

August 20, 1977

The U.S. spacecraft *Voyager 2* is launched to collect information about Jupiter and Saturn. *Voyager 1* follows on September 5, but on a faster path. It will reach Jupiter first.

March 5, 1979

Voyager 1 gets close to Jupiter and sends images of the planet back to Earth.

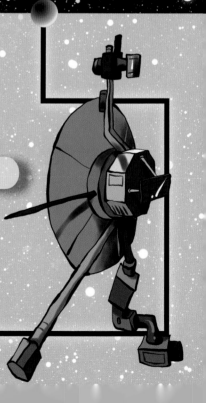

December 9, 1978

The U.S. *Pioneer Venus Multiprobe* maps the surface of Venus.

September 1, 1979

The U.S. space probe *Pioneer* 11 takes the first close-up pictures of Saturn.

February 14, 1980

The U.S. *Solar Maximus Mission* is launched. The satellite's job is to study bursts of energy on the sun called flares.

July 9, 1979

Voyager 2 reaches Jupiter.

April 12, 1981

The *Columbia* shuttle is launched by the United States. It is the world's first reusable space vehicle. Over the next 20 years or so, *Columbia* will go on 28 missions.

LIVING IN SPACE

June 18, 1983

Sally Ride becomes the first U.S. woman to travel in space. She is a crew member aboard the space shuttle *Challenger*.

► March 1, 1982

The Soviet probe *Venera* 13 provides the first Venus soil testing.

April 19, 1982

The *Salyut 7*, a Soviet space station, is launched.

211 DAYS
we're coming home!

May 13, 1982

Cosmonauts aboard the *Soyuz T-5* become the first team to live in the *Salyut 7* space station. They set a time record of 211 days.

January 24, 1986

Voyager 2 takes the first close-up photographs of Uranus and its moon. The spacecraft was launched by the United States in 1977.

moon

February 20, 1986

The Soviet Union launches the first part, or module, of Mir. Mir is the largest space station to date.

The National Informer

CHALLENGER EXPLODES!

January 28, 1986

The U.S. space shuttle *Challenger* explodes shortly after take-off. Everyone on board is killed, including teacher Christa McAuliffe.

A TELESCOPE IN SPACE

December 29, 1987

Cosmonaut Yuri Romanenko sets a record by spending 326 days in space.

August 10, 1990

The U.S. spacecraft *Magellan* starts a four-year mapping project of the planet Venus.

April 24, 1990

The U.S. space shuttle *Discovery* launches the Hubble Space Telescope. The telescope is a little longer than an average school bus.

August 25, 1989

The U.S. spacecraft *Voyager 2* orbits close to Neptune and takes photographs.

October 6, 1990

The U.S. spacecraft *Ulysses* begins its study of the sun.

February 3, 1994

Sergei Krikalev becomes the first Russian to fly on a U.S. space shuttle.

October 29, 1991

The U.S. spacecraft *Galileo* makes the first flyby of an asteroid.

December 2, 1993

The U.S. space shuttle *Endeavour* provides the first service call to the Hubble Space Telescope.

SPACE RECORDS

February 3, 1995

Eileen Collins, aboard the U.S. space shuttle *Discovery*, becomes the first woman to pilot a shuttle.

May 18, 1996

The X PRIZE Foundation announces a contest worth $10 million. The goal is to build a privately funded spacecraft and launch and land it twice.

$10,000,000

March 22, 1995

Cosmonaut Valeri Polyakov breaks the record for the longest stay in space. He spent 437 days at the Mir space station.

July 4, 1997

The U.S. probe *Mars Pathfinder* lands on Mars. It is a new kind of low-cost exploration device.

October 29, 1998

John Glenn, the first U.S. astronaut to orbit Earth, returns to space 36 years later.

December 4, 1998

The United States delivers *Unity*, the second part of the *International Space Station*.

ASSEMBLY INSTRUCTIONS FOR the INTERNATIONAL Space Station

Part TWO UNITY

October 15, 1997

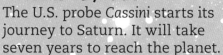

The U.S. probe *Cassini* starts its journey to Saturn. It will take seven years to reach the planet.

November 20, 1998

Russia delivers *Zarya*, the first part of the *International Space Station*.

TOURING SPACE

March 23, 2001

Mir is taken out of its orbit. Most of the space station burns up as it re-enters Earth's atmosphere. Large pieces fall into the Pacific Ocean.

November 2, 2000

The first crew arrives to live aboard the *International Space Station*. The three-man crew (one U.S. astronaut and two cosmonauts) will stay 136 days.

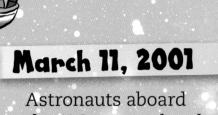

March 11, 2001

Astronauts aboard the U.S. space shuttle *Discovery* set a new spacewalking record: 8 hours and 56 minutes.

April 28, 2001

Dennis Tito becomes the first tourist in space. His ride aboard a Russian spacecraft costs $20 million.

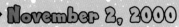

February 1, 2003

The U.S. space shuttle *Columbia* breaks apart while re-entering Earth's atmosphere. All crew members on board are killed.

e-Alert

Space Shuttle Columbia Disaster

Tragic End to Mission

June 13, 2002

Astronomers discover a Jupiter-like planet orbiting a faraway sun-like star. The find suggests that solar systems like ours exist elsewhere.

August 20, 2002

The U.S. spacecraft *Voyager 1* becomes the most distant human-created object in space. Launched in 1977, it has traveled about 8 billion miles (13 billion km).

October 15, 2003

Yang Liwei becomes the first man in space from China.

PRIVATE SPACE FLIGHT

January 3, 2004

The U.S. rover *Spirit* parachutes and bounces onto Mars. It begins its exploration of the planet.

September 29, 2004

SpaceShipOne makes its first attempt at winning the X PRIZE.

January 25, 2004

Opportunity, the sister rover to *Spirit*, joins the mission to explore Mars.

WELCOME to the Red Planet

N328KF

June 21, 2004

SpaceShipOne makes the first manned private space flight. It is a test flight for the X PRIZE contest, announced in 1996.

July 4, 2005

The U.S. probe *Deep Impact* slams into the Tempel 1 comet so scientists can review the debris.

July 26, 2005

Discovery becomes the first U.S. space shuttle launched after the *Columbia* disaster, in 2003.

October 4, 2004

SpaceShipOne makes its second flight into space and wins the $10 million X PRIZE. The craft was built by Burt Rutan.

August 16, 2005

Sergei Krikalev sets a world record by spending a total of 803 days in space.

THE FUTURE OF SPACE EXPLORATION

January 14, 2008

The U.S. spacecraft *Messenger* completes a flyby of Mercury and gives the first clear pictures of the planet.

August 8, 2007

Barbara Morgan, aboard the U.S. space shuttle *Endeavour*, becomes the first teacher in space.

September 13, 2007

A $30 million Google Lunar X PRIZE contest is announced. The goal is to launch a robot to the moon and send images back.

May 25, 2008

The U.S. *Phoenix Mars Lander* begins sending pictures from Mars. Its mission is to study the history of water on the planet.

April 15, 2010

U.S. President Barack Obama announces plans to send people to Mars by the year 2030.

2010

The U.S. space shuttle program is set to retire.

October 11, 2010

The NASA Authorization Act of 2010 becomes law. It sets many goals, including the development of new vehicles to replace space shuttles.

PLANS FOR THE NEXT GENERATION OF SPACE VEHICLES

June 18, 2009

The U.S. *Lunar Reconnaissance Orbiter* begins mapping the surface of the moon.

February 24, 2011

Discovery, NASA's oldest space shuttle, begins its 39th, and final, mission.

June 4, 2010

SpaceX, a private company, launches the *Falcon* 9 rocket. The rocket will provide business-related missions to the *International Space Station*.

BUILD YOUR OWN TIMELINE

A timeline represents a number of events in chronological order—the order in which they happened in time. This book has shown you what's happened in space exploration so far. Now create a timeline based on space exploration happening today.

Start with the last date in this book and take the timeline to present day. The World Almanac is a good source of information about aerospace. Also check the NASA Web site or search online for "space timeline" or "space exploration timeline for kids."

February 24, 2011

?

TODAY

Glossary

asteroid belt—the space between Mars and Jupiter

astronaut—a person trained for space flight

astronomer—a scientist who studies objects in space

atmosphere—the layer of gases surrounding a planet

comet—a space mass made of ice and dust that orbits the sun; comets appear to have long tails

cosmonaut—an astronaut of the Soviet or Russian space program

flyby—the close flight of a spacecraft past an object in space

launch—to send off

lunar module—a vehicle used to take astronauts from the main space module to the moon's surface and back

magnetic field—an area in which a pulling (magnetic) or electrical force can be found

nebula—a cloud of gas or dust in space

orbit—to circle around an object; also, the path or circle made by one object around another

probe—a device used to explore outer space

satellite—an object that orbits a planet or other space object

supernova—a star that explodes, giving off dazzling light

TO LEARN MORE

More Books to Read

Harris, Joseph. *Space Exploration: Impact of Science and Technology*. Pros and Cons. Pleasantville, N.Y.: Gareth Stevens Pub., 2010.

Jedicke, Peter. *Great Moments in Space Exploration*. Scientific American. New York: Chelsea House, 2007.

Stott, Carole. *Space Exploration*. DK Eyewitness Books. New York: Dorling Kindersley, 2010.

Internet Sites

FactHound offers a safe, fun way to find Internet sites related to this book. All of the sites on FactHound have been researched by our staff.

Here's all you do:

Visit *www.facthound.com*

Type in this code: 9781404866607

Super-cool stuff!

Check out projects, games and lots more at
www.capstonekids.com

INDEX

Look for all the books in the series:

An Illustrated Timeline of Inventions and Inventors
An Illustrated Timeline of Space Exploration
An Illustrated Timeline of Transportation
An Illustrated Timeline of U.S. States